Human Capital Management Report

Fiscal Year (FY) 2010

National Transportation Safety Board

Emily T. Carroll
Human Resources Officer
202-314-6233
Carrole@ntsb.gov

Barbara Zimmermann
Chief Human Capital Officer
December 15, 2010

Table of Contents

National Transportation Safety Board 1

Section I 4

    Introduction 4

Section II 6

    Executive Summary 6

    Strategic Alignment 6

    NTSB Human Capital Initiatives 7

    Governmentwide Initiatives 8

    Accountability 9

Section III 12

    NTSB Human Capital Initiatives 12

    Goals 12

    Actions 15

        Training 15

        Diversity 16

        Hiring System 16

        Competencies 17

        Records System 17

    Results 18

        Training 18

        Diversity 19

        Hiring System 20

        Competencies 21

        Records System 22

Section IV 24

    Governmentwide Initiatives 24

        Hiring Reform 24

        Worklife: Telework and Health and Wellness 27

        Employee Viewpoint Survey Action Planning 31

        Extension of Benefits to Same-Sex Domestic Partners of Federal Employees ... 34

        Managing Talent in Governmentwide Mission-Critical Occupations 35

        HCAAF System: Results-Oriented Performance Culture 37

Section V 45

    Accountability and Evaluation 45

Section VI 49

    Adjustments 49

Note: This report has been re-formatted for compliance with Section 508 of the Rehabilitation Act (29 U.S.C. 794d).

Section I

Introduction

The National Transportation Safety Board (NTSB) is pleased to submit its Human Capital Management Report for FY 2010, as required under 5 CFR Part 250. This report is the culmination of our annual human capital life cycle, which began with planning and goal-setting for the fiscal year; continued with the implementation of actions to recruit, develop, and retain a world-class workforce; and proceeded through an evaluation of program results and merit system compliance. OPM's Human Capital Assessment and Accountability Framework (HCAAF) is the conceptual model for this life cycle.

HCAAF Diagram

Relationship among HCAAF Systems

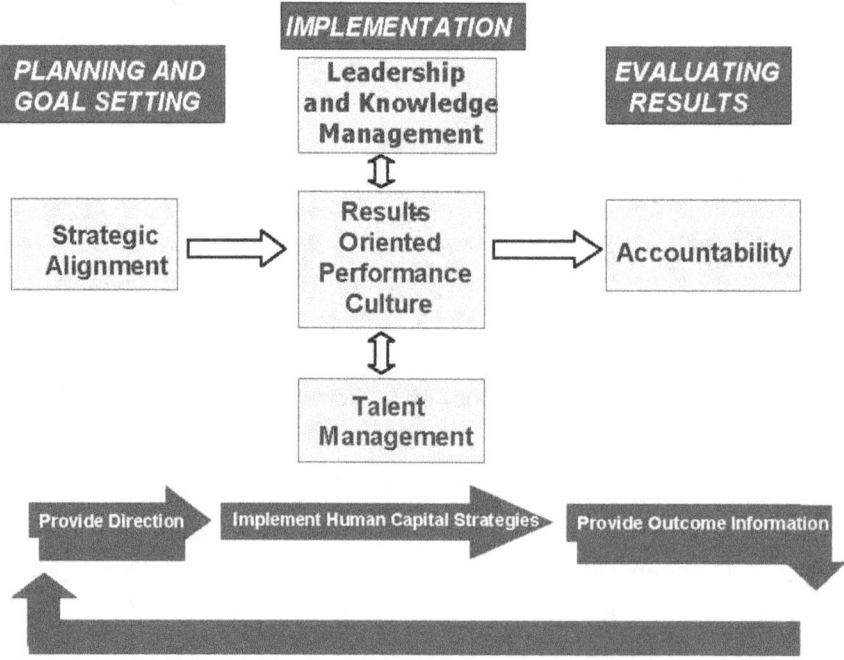

Our actions in assessing the NTSB's progress were guided by the NTSB Human Capital Accountability Policy (Operations Bulletin HRD-GEN-004), FYs 2009-2012 Human Capital Accountability System Plan, and the FY 2010 Human Capital Accountability Implementation Plan.

The following sections describe the NTSB's human capital goals and initiatives, the results achieved, and how the results are being used to make adjustments and improvements for the coming year. An overview of this report is presented below in the Executive Summary.

Section II

Executive Summary

The NTSB's first Strategic Human Capital Plan was issued July 17, 2008. Its publication initiated the agency's cycle of planning, implementing, and evaluating its human capital programs in alignment with the agency's Strategic Plan. During FY 2010, the NTSB continued to integrate its human capital management framework with the agency's business processes.

This second Human Capital Management Report is a status report on the agency's accomplishments during the preceding fiscal year, its work in progress, and its assessment of areas for continuing improvement. The report highlights NTSB initiatives, governmentwide initiatives, and focus areas under the HCAAF systems. This Executive Summary provides a brief overview of the topics covered in detail in the report.

Strategic Alignment

The NTSB's Strategic Human Capital Plan FY's 2008-2012 contains five goals:

Human Capital Goals

1. Align NTSB Human Capital strategic planning with the NTSB mission, NTSB strategic goals and objectives, office operating plans, performance plans, and the budget and financial reporting processes (including performance accountability reports).

2. Build leadership and management skills for the long term, and develop the means to identify and capture critical organization knowledge.

3. Maintain a diverse, results-oriented, high-performing workforce and utilize a performance management system that effectively differentiates between high and low performance, linking individual/team/unit performance to organizational goals and desired results.

4. Identify and address critical competency gaps; recruit, hire, and retain employees with the skills necessary for mission accomplishment; and continue to strive for a diverse workforce that reflects the variety of American culture.

5. Ensure that there is effective human capital management in support of the NTSB Strategic Plan.

These five human capital goals are linked to three objectives in the agency's Strategic Plan for fiscal years 2007-2012:

- Maintain a competent and effective investigative workforce;
- Align and improve the NTSB management team; and
- Develop a Strategic Human Capital Plan.

An implementation plan was used to track the completion of actions described in the Strategic Human Capital Plan in FY 2010. Throughout the year, staff made steady progress toward achieving the plan's goals. Seventy-one percent of actions that were led by the Human Resources Division (HRD) or the Chief Human Capital Officer (CHCO) were completed in FY 2010, with all remaining actions either started or ongoing.

NTSB Human Capital Initiatives

The NTSB undertook several initiatives during the year, in addition to governmentwide initiatives, to achieve the agency's human capital goals and improve our effectiveness. The following table presents the list of the NTSB's FY 2010 initiatives:

FY 2010 NTSB Initiatives

- **Training:** Develop a Strategic Training and Development Plan to guide employee training and career development in alignment with agency goals and objectives.

- **Diversity:** Create a Diversity Task Force to identify improvements in the recruitment, development, and retention of a diverse, high-performing workforce.

- **Hiring System:** Implement USA Staffing to improve the efficiency and effectiveness of the hiring process.

- **Competencies:** Assess investigator competency gaps as a basis for strategic workforce planning.

- **Records System:** Implement electronic official personnel files (e-OPF) to increase efficiency in maintaining personnel records and to improve access for employees, managers, and HRD staff.

These initiatives span the three human capital implementation systems.

Governmentwide Initiatives

Many governmentwide initiatives were begun in 2010. The NTSB is a small agency, so we were able to implement most, but not all, of these initiatives. The following are discussed in greater detail in this report:

FY 2010 Governmentwide Initiatives

- Hiring Reform: Eliminate written essay-style questions (Knowledge, Skills, and Abilities [KSAs]); use category rating; allow individuals to apply with resumes and cover letters; notify applicants about their status; ensure manager responsibility and accountability for hiring; and improve the quality and speed of hiring.

- Worklife (Telework and Health and Wellness): Increase telework and enhance employee health and wellness.

- Employee Viewpoint Survey Action Planning: Develop and implement an action plan to improve employee engagement and satisfaction.

- Extension of Benefits to Same-Sex Domestic Partners of Federal Employees: Modify policy documents and communicate changes that extend benefits to same-sex domestic partners of Federal employees.

- Managing Talent in Governmentwide Mission-Critical Occupations: Use a strategic workforce planning approach to manage talent in the information technology (IT), acquisition, HRD, and leadership corps.

- HCAAF Implementation System: Present accomplishments for the results-oriented performance culture human capital system.

Accountability

The NTSB implemented the agency's Human Capital accountability policy through an annual implementation plan. Accountability activities included these:

- Monthly tracking of the completion of actions in the human capital implementation plan.

- Analysis of responses to the NTSB customer satisfaction survey for internal customers of agency support services, including HRD.

- Compilation of data gathered from office directors to document their organization's hiring and training needs as input for workforce planning.

- Analysis of data from the 2009 Annual Employee Survey and the 2010 Employee Viewpoint Survey.

- Analysis of the Executive Development, Management Development, and Upward Mobility Programs.

- Merit System compliance reviews of staffing actions and performance plans. Each case file that resulted from a hiring action was audited by the HRD specialist; the Team Leader for Recruitment and Staffing audited each certificate prior to finalizing the selection. All performance plans were reviewed to ensure compliance with regulations.

- Analysis of the Senior Executive Service (SES) performance management system in order to maintain certification.

- Analysis of the Senior Level (SL) performance management system in order to request certification.

- Analysis of progress in implementing the HRD SWAT Team action plan.

- Analysis of barriers to streamlining the hiring process, eliminating the requirement for applicants to write narratives addressing the KSAs needed for jobs, implementing category rating, allowing applicants to apply with a resume and cover letter, notifying applicants at four points during the hiring process, and ensuring manager involvement in hiring.

- Analysis of data from the Office of Personnel Management's (OPM) applicant and manager surveys.

- Analysis of the hiring timeline.

- Analysis of the effectiveness of targeted outreach activities to attract diverse, highly qualified job applicants.

- Analysis of the National Resources Specialist (NRS) position as a unique requirement for carrying out mission-critical work.

- Analysis of workforce demographic data.

- Analysis of barriers to building a more diverse workforce.

- Analysis of data from the assessment of investigator competencies to identify gaps.

- Analysis of the awards program.

- Assessment of the general schedule (GS) performance management system using OPM's performance appraisal assessment tool (PAAT).

- Analysis of the systems, standards, and metrics data.

- Analysis of end-to-end hiring metrics.

- Quality reviews of official personnel files in preparation for conversion to electronic files.

- Completion of the annual training needs assessment.

Results of these analyses were used to identify actions and targets to implement in the Strategic Human Capital Plan in FY 2011. The actions for the coming year emphasize closing competency gaps for staff in mission-critical occupations; continuing development of the leadership corps; continuing improvements to involve managers and supervisors in workforce planning and hiring, streamline the hiring process, and improve the experience of applicants for NTSB jobs; and better integrating human capital assessment activities into the agency's business processes.

The NTSB is very limited in the staff resources it can devote to supporting human capital programs; this reality challenges the agency's ability to achieve its human capital goals. FY 2010 was a year in which the agency received an increase in its authorized full time equivalent (FTE) level. As a result, the number of hiring actions increased even as the agency was working to implement hiring reform. To handle this additional workload, the NTSB acquired additional contract personnel.

By undertaking initiatives to make improvements in all of the human capital systems, the NTSB is making continuing progress on achieving all five of its human capital goals. The following sections of this report describe this progress.

Ranking seventh among small agencies for positive employee responses to the Federal Employee Viewpoint Survey, the NTSB was recognized in FY 2010 by the Partnership for Public Service and American University's Institute for the Study of Public Policy Implementation as a Best Place to Work.

Section III

NTSB Human Capital Initiatives

In FY 2010, the NTSB identified several initiatives that were designed to continue the agency's progress in effective human capital management linked to the Strategic Plan. A discussion of the agency's overarching goals in the Strategic Plan and the Strategic Human Capital Plan provides the context for the subsequent discussion of these initiatives.

Goals

The NTSB Strategic Human Capital Plan FY's 2008-2012 was completed in July 2008. It contains five human capital goals that are linked to the mission and Strategic Plan.

> **The NTSB's mission is to promote transportation safety by**

- Maintaining our congressionally mandated independence and objectivity

- Conducting objective, precise accident investigations and safety studies

- Performing fair and objective airman and mariner certification appeals

- Advocating and promoting NTSB safety recommendations

- Assisting victims of transportation accidents and their families.

Of the four goals in the Strategic Plan FY's 2007-2012, two have objectives that link directly to the Strategic Human Capital Plan:

- Strategic Goal 1. Accomplish Objective Investigations of Transportation Accidents to Identify Issues and Actions that Improve Transportation Safety

    o Objective 2. Maintain a competent and effective investigative workforce and

- Strategic Goal 4. Organizational Excellence
  - ○ Objective 2. Align and improve the NTSB management team
  - ○ Objective 3. Develop a Strategic Human Capital Plan

The five goals in the Strategic Human Capital Plan that flow from the Strategic Plan and that align with the Human Capital Assessment and Accountability Framework (HCAAF) are these:

- **Human Capital Goal 1**. Align NTSB Human Capital strategic planning with the NTSB mission, NTSB strategic goals and objectives, office operating plans, performance plans; and the budget and financial reporting processes (including the performance accountability reports).

- **Human Capital Goal 2**. Build leadership and management skills for the long term and develop the means to identify and capture critical organization knowledge.

- **Human Capital Goal 3**. Maintain a diverse, results-oriented, high-performing workforce and utilize a performance management system that effectively differentiates between high and low performance, linking individual/team/unit performance to organizational goals and desired results.

- **Human Capital Goal 4**. Identify and address critical competency gaps; recruit, hire and retain employees with the skills necessary for mission accomplishment; and continue to strive for a diverse workforce that reflects the variety of American culture.

- **Human Capital Goal 5**. Ensure there is effective human capital management in support of the NTSB Strategic Plan.

In FY 2010, the NTSB undertook agency-specific initiatives for Human Capital Goals 2, 3, and 4, which link with the implementation of HCAAF systems for Leadership and Knowledge Management, Results-Oriented Performance Culture, and Talent Management, as shown below.

Human Capital Management Goals and Related FY 2010 Initiatives

Leadership and Knowledge Management

Human Capital Goal 2. Build leadership and management skills for the long term and develop the means to identify and capture critical organization knowledge.

FY 2010 Initiative

- **Training:** Develop a Strategic Training and Development Plan to guide employee training and career development in alignment with agency goals and objectives.

Results-Oriented Performance Culture

Human Capital Goal 3. Maintain a diverse, results-oriented, high-performing workforce and utilize a performance management system that effectively differentiates between high and low performance, linking individual/team/unit performance to organizational goals and desired results.

FY 2010 Initiative

- **Diversity:** Create a Diversity Task Force to identify improvements in the recruitment, development, and retention of a diverse, high-performing workforce.

Talent Management

Human Capital Goal 4. Identify and address critical competency gaps; recruit, hire and retain employees with the skills necessary for mission accomplishment; and continue to strive for a diverse workforce that reflects the variety of American culture.

FY 2010 Initiatives

- **Hiring System:** Implement USA Staffing to improve the efficiency and effectiveness of the hiring process.

- **Competencies:** Assess Investigator Competency Gaps as a basis for strategic workforce planning.

- **Records System**: Implement e-OPF to increase efficiency in maintaining personnel records and to improve access for employees, managers, and HRD staff.

Actions

Implementation of actions to achieve human capital initiatives in FY 2010 was tracked monthly on a spreadsheet that linked goals and objectives with associated outcomes, actions, target dates, and accountability. The status of initiatives was color-coded: Green indicated actions that were complete; Yellow, actions in progress or ongoing; and Red, actions not yet started. Each month, the percentage of actions completed was reported to agency management and discussed with the CHCO.

The following actions, arranged by initiative, were completed or implemented on an ongoing basis in FY 2010:

Training

Develop a Strategic Training and Development Plan to guide employee training and career development in alignment with agency goals and objectives.

- Set the strategic direction for training and development based on the Strategic Human Capital Plan and the Strategic Plan.

- Identify internal and external drivers of training needs.

- Review budget constraints and identify opportunities to maximize available resources.

- Complete the annual training needs assessment and establish individual and group training priorities.

- Identify long-range training goals and short-term actions to meet them.

- Research training delivery methods and sources to meet agency needs.

- Document evaluation plans to provide regular assessments and feedback for continuous improvement.

- Write a draft Strategic Training and Development Plan for agency review and implementation in FY 2011.

Diversity

Create a Diversity Task Force to identify improvements in the recruitment, development, and retention of a diverse, high-performing workforce.

- Assemble the Diversity Task Force membership from throughout the agency in response to the Chairman's initiative.

- Develop and adopt a Charter to guide the work of the Task Force.

- Conduct analysis of NTSB workforce demographics.

- Divide the membership into working groups for recruitment, career development and retention, and cultural awareness and diversity training.

- Review agency policies, procedures, and accomplishments.

- Identify areas for improvement and develop recommendations.

- Document recommendations for consideration by the Chairman.

- Develop action plans to implement recommendations.

- Communicate the recommendations to the agency and establish an Intranet portal to house the action plan and status updates on the completion of actions.

- Integrate actions with performance plans of executives, managers, and supervisors, as appropriate.

- Evaluate results.

Hiring System

Implement USA Staffing to improve the efficiency and effectiveness of the hiring process.

- Plan a phased implementation of USA Staffing, beginning with administrative positions.

- Participate in training at OPM.

- Communicate plans to agency leaders and to the union.

- Work in partnership with hiring managers to implement USA Staffing.

- Evaluate the effectiveness of the software for managing the flow of applications and for assessing applicants.

- Develop standard operating procedures for the Recruitment Team.
- Review the Operations Bulletin on Merit Staffing (policy) to identify changes and update as needed.
- Integrate the implementation of USA Staffing to improve hiring procedures.

Competencies

Assess Investigator Competency Gaps as a basis for strategic workforce planning.

- Complete the development of an investigator competency model through a series of review-and-comment opportunities for technical supervisors, managers, executives, and staff.
- Research available software systems to conduct an online assessment.
- Complete programming to adapt survey software for competency assessment.
- Develop and implement a communication plan.
- Conduct an online self-assessment with the investigator workforce.
- Conduct an online needs assessment with technical executives, managers, and supervisors.
- Analyze the data to identify competency gaps.
- Document the results.
- Discuss the findings with each technical office and share them with the workforce.
- Share the results with the Training Center for their use in planning training.
- Use the results as input to the Strategic Workforce Plan.

Records System

Implement e-OPF to increase efficiency in maintaining personnel records and to improve access for employees, managers, and HRD staff.

- Make contractual arrangements for scanning and converting paper Official Personnel Files (OPF) to electronic format.

- Complete a project plan and identify resource needs.

- Complete a quality review of each personnel folder, purging documents not required for inclusion in OPFs as defined by OPM's Guide to Recordkeeping.

- Assemble and package the OPFs for transfer to the scanning facility.

- Maintain secure controls to protect the information throughout the conversion process.

- Monitor the work of the scanning contractor and test the accuracy of completed electronic records.

- Establish protocols to manage electronic access to the e-OPFs.

- Train the HRD staff.

- Implement the communication plan, informing executives, managers, supervisors, and staff about the project and the benefits of electronic personnel records.

- Provide access to e-OPFs, as appropriate and in accordance with the established protocol.

- Scan incoming paper records, as needed, for inclusion in the e-OPFs.

Results

The following narrative presents the results of the NTSB's FY 2010 human capital initiatives.

Training

Develop a Strategic Training and Development Plan to guide employee training and career development in alignment with agency goals and objectives.

The NTSB has provided training and developmental opportunities to its workforce as a means of developing and maintaining the expertise needed to effectively carry out the agency's mission. With the creation of a Training Academy—later called the Training Center—the agency sought to consolidate its technical training and workforce development in an environment that would foster the exchange of ideas and knowledge. The Training Center conducts training needs assessments to identify emerging needs and to update its curriculum. Courses are routinely evaluated by participants, and higher levels of evaluation (following the Kirkpatrick model) are accomplished with the help of office directors to ensure that the training has been effective in improving the competence of employees.

In FY 2010, NTSB staff wrote the agency's first Strategic Training and Development Plan (STDP) to express the linkage between the strategic goals of the agency and the training and development program. The STDP includes analysis of workforce demographics and competency gaps, and it discusses the actions the NTSB will take to maintain mission-critical competencies into the future.

The STDP is undergoing final review during the first quarter of FY 2011 and is expected to be published by the end of the calendar year. Implementation will begin immediately.

Results from the 2010 Employee Viewpoint Survey show that 67 percent of respondents agree that they are given a real opportunity to improve their skills (Q.1) and 77 percent feel they have enough information to do their job well (Q.2). Respondents were less positive regarding their satisfaction with training (Q. 68: 50 percent positive) and less confident that their training needs were assessed (Q. 18: 53 percent positive).

Diversity

Create a Diversity Task Force to identify improvements in the recruitment, development, and retention of a diverse, high-performing workforce.

As a result of the work of the cross-agency Diversity Task Force, the NTSB realized several key accomplishments:

- The agency adopted a common definition of diversity and the Chairman issued a Diversity Policy memorandum to all employees in June 2010.

- A Diversity Action Plan was developed and implemented. All employees can track the agency's progress in meeting its goals by visiting the Intranet webpage.

- The FY 2011 Operating Plan includes diversity and outreach performance measures.

- Diversity and outreach measures are included in the performance plans of all senior executives.

- A diversity training contract was awarded.

- Training plans for FY 2011 courses on diversity were approved.

- A Senior Advisor for Workforce Operations position was established and filled.

- A review of the Management Development and Upward Mobility programs was begun.

- A Diversity Blog was established on the Intranet, allowing two-way communication.

- The NTSB held a slogan contest, involving the entire staff.

Implementation of the Action Plan will continue in FY 2011, with organizational changes to strengthen the Office for EEO, Diversity, and Inclusion; revitalization of the plan for marketing agency positions; development of a training year budget that spans fiscal years; review of agency policies regarding payment to maintain professional accreditations; and other changes to agency hiring, placement, training, and development programs.

Hiring System

Implement USA Staffing to improve the efficiency and effectiveness of the hiring process.

The NTSB purchased USA Staffing for use beginning in FY 2010. Because the agency had experienced problems in implementing another automated staffing product several years ago, HRD's leadership decided to implement USA Staffing in phases to demonstrate the value of the software for improving the hiring process. The implementation strategy included frequent communication with senior leaders and with the union to understand and address their concerns and to build partnerships for success.

HRD began the implementation of USA Staffing with job opportunity announcements (JOA) for summer employment for students and for HRD positions. The staff learned to use the system as they advertised these jobs and processed the resulting applications. This learning was critical because the software soon became an integral part of implementing the President's Hiring

Reform Initiative. As HRD was working to reform the hiring process, its hiring workload increased dramatically. As a result, the agency was allotted additional positions to carry out its mission-critical work.

Hiring managers prioritized their staffing needs in order to focus hiring efforts appropriately. This prioritization helped HRD to design the work groups of managers that would develop alternative assessments to replace KSAs.

Implementation of USA Staffing continued to expand throughout the year for use in staffing administrative (non-mission-critical) positions. Mission-critical positions are being considered for transition to the software system as technical hiring managers express their willingness to use it.

Competencies

Assess Investigator Competency Gaps as a basis for strategic workforce planning.

Beginning in 2009, the NTSB laid the foundation for strategic workforce planning for the accident investigator workforce, which comprises over 50 percent of the agency's positions, by drafting a competency model. This workforce includes individuals in a variety of technical and professional occupations:

- Accident Investigator (GS-1801)
- Air Safety Investigator (GS-1815)
- Engineer (GS-0801-0899)
- Psychologist (Human Performance) (0180)
- Railroad Safety Specialist (GS-2121)
- Scientist (Chemist, Metallurgist, Meteorologist) (GS-1301-1399)
- Transportation Specialist (GS-2101)

In 2010, the competency model was completed with the help of managers, supervisors, and investigators. A survey tool was adapted for the purpose of conducting an online self-assessment by investigators and a needs assessment by managers and supervisors. This assessment was completed in June 2010.

Analysis of the gaps between the supply (workforce competency level) and the demand (needs assessment) revealed that nearly all competencies are present at the appropriate levels in the workforce. At least one individual considers him/herself an "expert" for each competency. However, a few gaps exist across all investigators and within grade levels and technical offices.

The following gaps in mission-critical competencies were identified across all key occupations and grade levels:

- Change Agent
- Resource Management
- External Awareness

A separate analysis by grade level across all key occupations showed two additional competency gaps:

- Meeting Management
- Survival Factors

These identified competency gaps are being considered in plans for the training and development program over the next few years. Further analyses revealed that additional training would be beneficial in writing, information management, and project management.

The achievement of the milestone to complete a competency gap analysis of the accident investigator workforce was a significant accomplishment. The project not only provided actionable data for meeting the training needs of the staff, it also introduced the concept of competency-based human resources systems at a time when hiring reform would demand streamlined assessments of the competencies of applicants for agency jobs.

The NTSB is building on this assessment by providing detailed analyses to each technical office for its use in projecting its hiring and training needs. In addition, the agency is using the competency data along with analysis of workforce demographic data to complete its first strategic workforce plan, which will be released in FY 2011.

Records System

Implement e-OPF to increase efficiency in maintaining personnel records and to improve access for employees, managers, and HRD staff.

The NTSB completed the successful conversion of paper employee OPFs to electronic format during FY 2010. By following a detailed project plan, HRD staff completed the review of all employee personnel files, packaged and shipped the records securely, monitored the scanning and conversion process, made corrections as needed, and provided electronic access to staff members as appropriate. An ongoing communication plan guided the HRD staff's efforts to inform executives, managers, supervisors, and staff members throughout the agency about the benefits of this new system of records.

Section IV

Governmentwide Initiatives

Hiring Reform

Actions to improve the hiring process resulted initially from the work done in FY 2009 by the HRD SWAT Team. That team, which consisted of agency managers and HRD staff members, analyzed the hiring timeline to identify barriers to reducing the time to hire in alignment with the End-to-End (E2E) (80-day) hiring model. The outcome of this analysis was the action plan that was included in last year's Human Capital Management Report. In addition, the HRD SWAT Team developed streamlined templates for JOAs for the following mission-critical occupations:

- Investigator (GS-1801)

- Air Safety Investigator (GS-1815)

- Transportation Specialist (GS-2101)

- Railroad Specialist (GS-2121)

- Aerospace Engineer (GS-0861)

During the year, the NTSB made progress on the actions plan developed by the HRD SWAT Team:

- The CHCO led the offices in projecting their hiring needs for the next 2 years, which resulted in the establishment of agency-level hiring priorities and an allocation plan to guide managers on positions to fill.

- The hiring Plan Schedule (a "contract" between hiring managers and HRD) was revised to reflect the E2E hiring model.

- The approval process for hiring actions was revised to reinforce the requirement for approved position descriptions (PD), job analysis, and assessment strategy in advance of the decision to proceed.

- HRD has begun building a library of PDs, along with related documents, that will be available to managers online.

- Applicants are receiving timely notification of their status (receipt of application, qualifications for the job, certified for consideration, and selected or not selected) at those points in the process.

- A pilot study for implementing USA Staffing began and has continued to expand to manage the flow of applications throughout the hiring process, as the NTSB gains experience using the system.

- HRD began testing automated assessment for some non-mission-critical vacancies in FY 2010.

With the launch of the President's Hiring Reform Initiative, the NTSB revised the action plan and expanded its scope.

- Senior executives received briefings on hiring reform and shared in plans to determine how the NTSB would implement it.

- HRD developed a category rating policy and guided it through the agency review and approval process.

- HRD delivered training to hiring managers covering the President's initiative and changes to the NTSB process, the new category rating policy, and procedures for selecting officials.

- HRD developed strategies to help hiring managers meet the new timeline, such as suggesting that calendars be blocked to reserve time for interviews when certificates of eligibles were expected to be ready.

- HRD acquired additional resources by filling a position and by obtaining contractors who could help meet the short-term need for HRD staff.

- Hiring managers joined working groups to develop assessments to replace KSA essays.

- HRD began development of an Intranet-housed PD library and other tools and job aids for hiring managers.

- HRD modified JOA templates to eliminate KSAs and allow job seekers to apply with a resume and cover letter.

- HRD continued to expand the use of USA Staffing to manage the flow of applications and to assess applicants.

- HRD analyzed manager feedback and made adjustments in the process, as needed.

Results, to date, have been promising. Hiring managers have adapted to the new procedures and are working in active partnership with their HRD consultants. This partnership is expected to show improvements in the responses of hiring managers to the CHCO Manager Satisfaction Survey. In FY 2010, responses were few (7). Of those who responded, one-third reported involvement in workforce planning, while 57 percent were satisfied with the competencies of applicants referred for the job. Time-to-hire data showed improvement: The total number of days spent for hiring individuals through the delegated examining process decreased from 176 days in FY 2009 to 129 days in FY 2010. More progress is expected over the coming year.

In FY 2011, HRD will provide a number of training opportunities to hiring managers to increase their understanding of their role, the human capital flexibilities that they can use to hire the "best and the brightest," and how HRD can support them at each stage from workforce planning through orientation of new employees.

Worklife: Telework and Health and Wellness

The NTSB offers many policies and programs to improve the quality of employees' work and lives, as well as their health and wellness. With flexible work schedules and a well-established teleworking program, the agency supports employees' ability to be the most productive while balancing work and personal demands.

The agency's telework policy is contained in Operations Bulletin HRD-GEN-003. The policy specifies eligibility criteria, roles and responsibilities, and procedures for implementing telework on a project basis, or through a full-time or part-time permanent arrangement. Each office provides a quarterly report to the telework coordinator in the Office of Human Resources who oversees the program and fulfills internal and external reporting requirements. E-mail distribution lists have been established for full-time and part-time teleworkers as a means of improving communication.

The NTSB makes extensive use of telework: The agency currently has 41 full-time and 108 part-time teleworkers; combined, they make up 38.5 percent of the total NTSB workforce (385). Employee Viewpoint Survey results for 2010 demonstrate positive views of the NTSB telework program: 73 percent of respondents expressed satisfaction with teleworking.

Similarly, the NTSB offers a robust health and wellness program to provide employees with information in various formats:

- An annual health benefits fair
- Seminars on health and wellness topics (2010)
    - Long Term Care
    - Nutrition, including individual counseling and measurement of Body Mass Index
    - Stress Management
- Tabletop presentations, including question and answer sessions, during health benefits open season
- Presentations on health and wellness programs given at office-level meetings

- "HRD Advisory" online newsletter covering health and wellness topics, including changes coming as a result of Heath Care Reform and recent retirement system changes (2010).

The NTSB partners with the nearby headquarters of the U.S. Deparment of Housing and Urban Development to provide employees with fitness center and health unit services. The NTSB also provides a subsidy for employee fitness club monthly expenses and offers periodic health screenings.

NTSB offices have automated external defibrillators available for first-aid emergencies. The agency's Occupational Safety and Health Program recently established a cross-agency advisory committee to protect employees from work-related hazards.

To increase employee involvement in wellness activities, the agency sponsored summer and fall walking groups. Participants were challenged to "walk to the beach" or "walk to see the pretty leaves." Walkers report their weekly totals to an e-mail account (NTSBwalker). Results were announced agency-wide, and participants celebrated their success and posed for a group photo. Thirty-five employees participated in the summer, and 19 participated in the fall.

Five elements of a worksite wellness program (health education, integration, linkages with related programs, screening, and supportive social and physical environments) were evaluated to develop a wellness implementation plan. The table below captures the highlights of this plan, which is designed to achieve an employee participation rate in wellness activities over the next 5 years of 75 percent:

Table 1: NTSB CY11 Action Plan to Improve Employee Participation in Wellness Activities

Objective	Element	Action	Responsible
Increase participation of the field staff members in health education.	Health Education	Use videoconference capability to make health education seminars available to field staff members.	HRD/AD
Explore senior management interest in a pilot program to grant the use of duty time for participation in wellness activities.	Integration	Research regulatory/policy requirements and present for senior management consideration.	HRD/MD/GC
Identify opportunities to link health and wellness information sessions.	Linkages with related programs	Benchmark the experience of other small agencies.	HRD
Offer wellness screenings, as available	Screenings	Identify wellness screenings available at little or no cost.	HRD
Identify ways to enhance the social and physical environment	Supportive Social and Physical Environ- ments	Explore options for improving the social and physical environment during planned renovations.	AD/HRD

Employee Survey Results (2010) for telework and for health and wellness topics are shown in the chart below. Fifty-five percent of respondents report satisfaction with health and wellness programs, and 57 percent report that they are satisfied with the Employee Assistance Program. Child care and elder care programs received mainly neutral responses and small favorable and unfavorable responses, indicating the need for more information to be available as employees' life stages change.

The following chart was generated by an analytic tool developed by the Partnership for Public Service and the Hay Group to assist agencies in understanding their 2010 Employee Viewpoint Survey results.

Partnership for Public Service • Best Places to Work Study

Report for: National Transportation Safety Board

Question Summary: Question Order (Ascending)

	Valid N	% Fav	% Neut	% Unfav	2009 Trend	Total Agency	Total Gov	Private Sector
					% Favorable Difference			
Family Friendly Culture	--	45	45	10	-40	--	+4	--
73 How satisfied are you with teleworking?	224	73	17	10	+6	--	+39	--
74 How satisfied are you with alternative work schedules (AWS)?	225	87		12	+2	--	+25	--
75 How satisfied are you with health and wellness programs (for example, exercise, medical screening, quit smoking programs)	214	55	35	10	--	--	0	--
76 How satisfied are you with the employee assistance program (EAP)?	167	57	38	5	--	--	+11	--
77 How satisfied are you with child care programs (for example, daycare, parenting classes, parenting support groups)?	97	11	71	18	--	--	-13	--
78 How satisfied are you with elder care programs (for example, support groups, speakers)?	99	16	68	16	--	--	-3	--

Employee Viewpoint Survey Action Planning

Since 2004, employees at the NTSB have participated in governmentwide human capital surveys. Response rates, above 60 percent each year, have demonstrated employees' interest in expressing their views to make the agency a better place to work. The response rate for the 2010 Employee Viewpoint Survey was 71 percent, which surpassed all previous years' levels of participation.

NTSB positive responses exceeded governmentwide results for 60 of the 78 questions (77 percent). The ten highest positive-ranked responses are indicated below. They center on job satisfaction, work/life, health and safety, performance, and mission accomplishment. The overall average positive response was 66.5 percent. Ranking seventh among small agencies, the NTSB was recognized by the Partnership for Public Service and American University's Institute for the Study of Public Policy Implementation as a Best Place to Work.

Table 2: Ten Highest Positive Reponses

% Positive	Item	Short Description
98.8	7	Willingness to put in extra effort
93.9	13	My work is important
92.8	39	Agency mission accomplishment
91.7	28	Quality of work of the team
90.8	8	Looking for ways to do my job better
90.5	74	Satisfaction with alternate work schedules (work/life)
89.6	12	Agency goals and priorities
88.9	5	Satisfaction with work
88.8	35	Protection from health & safety hazards
87.7	16	Accountability

Although the overall results of the 2010 survey indicated that employees are satisfied with their work and understand how they contribute to the agency's mission, there were some areas needing improvement. The NTSB analyzed the items with the lowest levels of positive response and identified five objectives that focused action should target. A summary table showing these objectives and actions is shown below.

Table 3: NTSB CY11 Action Plan to Improve Employee Engagement and Satisfaction

Objective	Survey Items*	Action	Responsible
Increase employee development opportunities.	11, 47	Identify tools that support managers and supervisors in managing the talent in their organizations.	Managers/ Supervisors/ Training Center/ HRD
Increase employee engagement in the workplace.	3, 32, 63	Engage NTSB employees in focus groups and forums to gather ideas on improving the workplace and increasing their engagement.	MD's Office/ HRD
Improve supervisory skill level and employee awareness in performance management.	22, 23, 24	Sponsor management and employee briefings on performance management and communication.	HRD
Improve employee skill level.	1, 18, 21, 27, 68	Work with the Training Center on group training opportunities.	Training Center/ HRD
Strengthen leadership competencies of current and aspiring leaders.	53, 64, 66	Continue developing leadership competencies.	Managers/ Training Center

A more detailed set of action plans, with an expanded set of actions for each of the objectives, will guide the NTSB's efforts over the coming year to increase employee engagement and satisfaction. Results from the 2011 Employee Viewpoint Survey will show the progress that is being made.

Extension of Benefits to Same-Sex Domestic Partners of Federal Employees

The NTSB updated its benefits information on the agency's Intranet site to implement the President's Memorandum Regarding Extension of Benefits to Same-Sex Domestic Partners of Federal Employees, using OPM guidance provided in June 2010. Through its FEDBENEFITS portal, the NTSB gives employees nationwide the latest information on Federal benefits with links to reference sites. Information extending benefits to same-sex domestic partners is shown for the Long Term Care program.

A representative from Long Term Care Partners gave three hour-long presentations during the year and offered one-on-one counseling to attendees. The sessions were webcast to ensure coverage for field staff members. Attendance was very good, with about 25 participants per session. In addition, Long Term Care Partners participated in the annual health fair (November) and was available to answer questions about the eligibility of employees and their family members, including same-sex domestic partners.

In FY 2011, the NTSB will provide employees with additional information about the extension of benefits to same-sex domestic partners through its e-mail "HRD Advisory" and its FEDBENEFITS portal.

Managing Talent in Governmentwide Mission-Critical Occupations

Managing talent for human resources, information technology, and acquisition, along with supporting the development and continuity of the organization's leadership corps, is critical to the continued success of the NTSB in carrying out its safety mission. In the same way that the agency conducts strategic workforce planning for its technical workforce, the NTSB projects its staffing needs for these occupations in light of the agency's strategic direction and governmentwide initiatives (the "demand"). Analysis of the current workforce bench strength and competency gaps provides the "supply" side of the equation.

In FY 2010, the makeup of the Human Resources staff changed, and it grew in size. Internal moves affected the positions of HRD chief and two of the three team leaders. A senior staff member retired; this vacancy was filled at the entry level as a means to build future capacity. With a sharp increase in the staffing workload (from an increase in the FTE ceiling) and the agency's action plan to implement hiring reform, the HRD staff was temporarily augmented with contract employees. HRD made changes to some staff members' assignments to provide for growth and development while meeting an expanding workload and to plan a smooth transition as one team leader moves into retirement. Several HRD positions have been advertised and are in the process of being filled. In the coming year, HRD will continue to focus on staff development and will use available human capital flexibilities to meet the division's changing needs.

The Office of the Chief Information Officer (OCIO) develops and maintains the NTSB's IT Strategic Plan. The plan includes a goal for IT workforce management, which guides the organization's planning and implementation of strategies to acquire, develop, and retain the staff resources needed to carry out the IT Strategic Plan. OCIO participates in the governmentwide analysis of competency gaps in the IT workforce, sponsored by the CIO Council. Employee Individual Development Plans (IDP) provide the means to close skills gaps by linking training and development opportunities to strategic goals. OCIO meets its staffing needs with a mix of Federal employees and contractors. Contractors bring up-to-date specialized skills and thus help update the knowledge of career employees. OCIO staffing remained stable in FY 2010. One IT specialist (GS-2210) was hired during the year.

The NTSB has an acquisition staff of six, with two Contract Specialists (GS-1102) in the grade range 11-12 and five in the grade range 13-15. During the year, the staff added one grade level 11 position, which was filled competitively in December.

The NTSB's leadership corps has maintained its effectiveness despite adjustments throughout the year as incumbents in several positions at the executive-, manager-, and supervisor-levels have changed. The number of senior executives has remained constant at 16. As of the end of the fiscal year, 2 of the 14 management positions were vacant and in the process of being filled. The agency has used its leadership development programs—, the Management Development Program and the Executive Leadership Development Program—to prepare a pool of individuals to compete for future leadership positions. In addition, executives, managers, and supervisors engage in individual development activities. As a result, successors have been prepared and ready to step into higher-level leadership positions as these positions become available.

HCAAF System: Results-Oriented Performance Culture

The NTSB continued to improve its results-oriented performance culture. The discussion below focuses on performance management. The agency's initiative to improve diversity is discussed in detail above.

The HCAAF System Standard and related NTSB Human Capital Goal provided the context for this year's accomplishments.

System Standard: The agency has a diverse, results-oriented, high-performing workforce and a performance management system that differentiates between high and low levels of performance and effectively links individual/team/unit performance to organizational goals and desired results.

Goal: Maintain a diverse, results-oriented, high-performing workforce and utilize a performance management system that effectively differentiates between high and low performance, linking individual/team/unit performance to organizational goals and desired results.

Highlights of actions and accomplishments are shown below, as are actions that have been identified for FY 2011:

Table 4: Highlights of actions and accomplishments

FY 10 Objectives	- Strengthen the existing performance management system. - Achieve full certification of the Senior Level (SL)/Scientific or Professional (ST) Performance Management System.
FY 10 Actions	- Complete Performance Appraisal Assessment Tool (PAAT). - Monitor use of new program and alignment with strategic goals. - Consider options for automating GS performance management program. - Develop more generic elements as needed. - Conduct training. - Meet with five organizations to discuss findings of Performance Evaluation Plan (PEP) standards review. - Continue to monitor compliance with program requirements. - Prepare package to request full certification of SL/ST performance management system.
FY 10 Results	- Completed draft PAAT assessment; report will be submitted to OPM in January 2011. - Reviewed PEPs to reveal that 100% of plans are aligned with strategic goals. - Reviewed available private sector and government-sponsored automated performance management systems; developed automated system requirements; and arranged for four automated performance management system demonstrations. - Developed generic PEPs for STEP/SCEP/ interns; developed two new generic performance elements for the mission-critical occupation of investigator (analysis and report writing); and one existing supervisory element was modified and one new generic element was established for HRD staff members who conduct hiring to fully implement the hiring reform initiative. - Conducted four supervisory training sessions on strategies for effectively monitoring and rating employee performance, and improving overall employee/supervisor communication and feedback. - Met with 11 organizations to discuss findings of PEP standards review. - Monitored program requirement compliance with supervisory certifications at designated phases of the process (achieved noteworthy increases in awards granted to employees in protected racial categories). - Full certification of SL/ST performance management system granted by OPM.
FY 11 Actions	- Finalize PAAT and submit to OPM for review (consider implementation of additional program activities based on review findings). - Work on developing additional generic elements for the agency's mission-critical occupations to incorporate competency assessment work efforts and team leader positions, and to emphasize results rather than activities. - Update agency GS Performance Management Operations Bulletin (policy) to strengthen and clarify program requirements. - Conduct supervisory training to move supervisors toward a more "results-oriented" focus. - Implement new hiring reform generic elements into calendar year 2011 PEPs. - Brief supervisors and managers on results of calendar year 2010 ratings both in terms of rating and awards distribution. - Conduct PAAT assessment of SES and SL/ST performance management systems.

Assessment

Performance Management Program

FY10 marked a period of general program stability for the GS performance management system implemented in January 2009. The agency elected to provide supervisors additional and more targeted assistance and guidance, rather than making additional changes to the system, which have been occurring over the past two appraisal cycles. During FY10, supervisors became more adept at using the performance management system, which is available in a point-and-click, SharePoint environment; some supervisors indicated that it only took them only 15 minutes to establish a new PEP for an employee. Supervisors also took advantage of and use more of the generic performance elements when establishing their PEPs. This resulted in a shift from time spent on establishing PEPs to increasing the amount of time that supervisors communicate with employees, which was one of the desired benefits of the system when it was implemented in 2009.

It is apparent that supervisors have been able to clearly understand and easily link their employees' performance elements to the agency's strategic goals. Supervisors also indicated that they are comfortable using and updating the automated PEPs, and have regularly responded to HRD-requested certifications that program requirements are being met.

Program Accomplishments

A number of noteworthy accomplishments in this program area occurred during FY10. For one, the agency conducted an extensive review of available private sector and government-sponsored automated performance management systems; developed automated system requirements; and arranged for and attended four automated performance management system demonstrations. It was determined that, although the agency would like to further automate its GS performance management approach beyond the SharePoint environment, the timing is not right at this time to do so (considering that this would be yet another change for supervisors). Accordingly, this effort has been postponed temporarily. With regard to generic performance elements, it was noted that 3 of the agency's 11 organizational entities use only such elements to identify and evaluate performance; over 95 percent of all employees are assessed against one or more generic elements. Since supervisors embrace the use of generic performance elements, additional such elements were developed for all Student Temporary Experience Program/Student Career Experience program (STEP/SCEP)/interns, two new generic performance elements were established for the mission-critical occupation of investigator (analysis and report writing), and one existing supervisory element was modified and one new generic element established for HRD staff members who conduct hiring.

In terms of outreach, four supervisory training sessions were conducted on strategies for effectively monitoring and rating employee performance and for improving overall employee/supervisor communication and feedback. Nearly 100 percent of supervisors attending the training sessions indicated that the training was effective in helping them perform their supervisory duties and responsibilities more effectively. Also, individual office interviews were conducted to discuss the findings of a 100-percent PEP standards review. Many supervisors asked followup questions and made substantive changes to their employees' PEPs as a result.

Finally, the agency monitored program-requirement compliance through the use of just-in-time reminders and requests for supervisory certifications. Followup was conducted with supervisors who had failed to respond or who had requested additional time to fully meet program requirements. The agency's SharePoint site addressing the GS performance management program is routinely updated with the latest program information and reminders of key performance requirements.

GS Performance Management Assessments

Two separate internal reviews were conducted in FY10: an end-of-appraisal-cycle review and a PAAT assessment.

The first end-of-appraisal-cycle review included a spot check of the final PEPs and noted that 100 percent of plans aligned with strategic goals. This review also examined the ratings and performance awards given to employees. Information from the 2009 cycle revealed that 53 percent of the workforce had been rated as outstanding; 40 percent had been rated as excellent, and 7 percent had been rated as Fully Successful. The 2009 appraisals, which were conducted in December 2009, resulted in more Outstanding performance ratings than those conducted in 2008. Employees receiving Outstanding ratings increased from 49.4 percent to 53 percent, decreasing Fully Successful ratings from 8.3 percent to 7 percent, and Excellent ratings from 42.3 percent to 41 percent. All racial groupings experienced the increase: Asians receiving Outstanding ratings increased from 29 percent to 69 percent, Blacks increased from 35 percent to 52 percent, Hispanic/Latinos increased from 33 to 43 percent, and Whites increased from 49 to 52 percent. In addition, 93 percent of employees eligible for a monetary performance award received one, up from 88 percent in 2008. However, the number of quality step increases awarded in 2009 (8 percent of monetary performance awards) was down from those given in 2008 (12 percent).

The second review conducted in FY10 was the agency's PAAT assessment. The conduct of this review was delayed in part due to the late receipt of the latest PAAT guidance from OPM. At this time this report is being submitted, the PAAT is still in draft form. It will be submitted to OPM in January 2011.

SES/SL Performance Management

In FY 2010, the NTSB received full certification of its performance management system for Senior Level (SL) and Scientific or Professional (ST) employees. The NTSB's SES performance management system had received full certification in FY 2009. Achievement of full certification for the SL/ST system met the target for one measure in the agency's Human Capital Implementation Plan:

- Submit required materials and request to OPM for SL/ST performance management system certification (Target = Y); Target met; obtained OMB concurrence and OPM approval for 2 years (full certification).

Operations Bulletin HRD-PRF-004 describes the policies and procedures governing the SL and ST Performance Management System. The operations bulletin was last updated and distributed to the staff via the Intranet on May 28, 2009. Prior to the establishment of a separate SL/ST performance management system in 2007, it had been addressed in Operations Bulletin HRD-PRF-001, which now applies only to the general workforce.

All NTSB employees were provided the FY 2010 annual organizational assessment in early October 2010, and rating officials incorporated both organizational and individual accomplishment considerations in the proposed annual SES and SL/ST performance ratings. The Performance Review Board (for SES) and the Performance Review Panel (for SL/ST) also were provided the annual organizational performance assessment prepared by the Office of Management and shared by the Senior Performance Official as an overview in considering performance appraisals, bonuses/awards, and any pay adjustments for senior executives and senior level employees.

The NTSB plans to continue to use the PAAT to assess its performance management programs for SES and SL/ST employees in FY 2011.

Improving Internal Communication

The NTSB also improved internal communication in FY 2010. Offices continued to carry out action plans to address feedback gained from the Communications Survey. Organizational-level communications were increased, building upon established vehicles such as online newsletters and regular e-mail communications from the Chairman, Board Members, and the Managing Director. FY 2010 saw the agency increase communications with the staff through All Hands meetings to discuss the new lease for office space, the schedule for renovations, and the impact on the staff throughout the process. All Hands meetings were accessible to field staff through the Web, and presentations and subsequent questions and answers were posted for all to access.

Results from the 2010 Employee Viewpoint Survey for Question #56. Managers communicate the goals and priorities of the organization show that employees view internal communications positively: Over the last four surveys, the positive response for this item was 64.6 percent (2010), 62.2 percent (2009), 69.0 percent (2008), and 62.0 percent (2007).

Employee Survey Results

The Results-Oriented Performance Culture Index from the 2010 Employee Viewpoint Survey was 64.1 percent, an increase from 2008 (62.2 percent) and higher than both the governmentwide average (54.0 percent) and the small agency average (60.0 percent). However, there continues to be room for improvement, as evidenced by the responses to items 22 (*Promotions are based on merit*—49.7 percent positive), 23 (*In my work unit, steps are taken to deal with a poor performer who cannot or will not improve*—38.9 percent positive), and 24 (*In my work unit, differences in performance are recognized in a meaningful way*—47.9 percent positive). As noted in the section of this report on Employee Viewpoint Survey Action Planning, the NTSB will be sponsoring management and employee briefings on performance management and communication to improve the skills of supervisors and raise the awareness of employees about these topics.

Diversity Management

The NTSB is making an agency-wide effort to improve diversity management, as discussed in above, through the work of the Diversity Task Force.

2011 Activity Focus

Actions in FY 2011 are designed to build on the progress that the NTSB has been making to improve its performance management systems and processes. The agency will continue its communication with, and support to, supervisors, managers, and executives to enhance their performance management. Additional generic elements for mission-critical occupations and the team leader role will be developed. Assessments of the SES and SL/ST performance

43

management systems will be conducted using the PAAT, and the assessment of the GS system will be finalized and submitted to OPM.

Analysis

The NTSB's performance culture continues to show progress towards a results orientation that links individual accomplishments with organizational achievements. The GS performance management system benefitted from the tools available through MS SharePoint to ease the administrative burden on managers. Through the use of generic standards and point-and-click technology, the focus of performance management shifted to communication about goals and feedback about accomplishments. The NTSB has built assessment into its ongoing implementation of performance management systems and will use the results obtained to continue making improvements in the future.

Efforts to improve internal communications and diversity management showed progress and will continue to be emphasized as integral to the agency's success.

Section V

Accountability and Evaluation

In FY 2009, the NTSB developed, documented, and implemented its Human Capital Accountability System. Using an annual accountability implementation plan, the agency assessed all human capital systems in FY 2010. The following table presents the measures taken to evaluate the effectiveness of actions toward achieving the human capital goals.

FY 2010 Accountability Activities

Strategic Alignment Human Capital Goal: Align NTSB Human Capital strategic planning with the following: The NTSB mission, NTSB strategic goals and objectives, Office Operating Plans, performance plans; and the budget and financial reporting processes (including the Performance Accountability Reports).

- Monthly tracking of the completion of actions in the human capital Implementation plan.

- Analysis of responses to NTSB customer satisfaction survey for internal customers of agency support services, including HRD.

- Compilation of data gathered from office directors to document their organization's hiring and training needs as input for workforce planning.

Leadership and Knowledge Management Human Capital Goal: Build leadership and management skills for the long term and develop the means to identify and capture critical organization knowledge.

- Analysis of data from the 2009 Annual Employee Survey and the 2010 Employee Viewpoint Survey.

- Identify gaps in leadership competencies.

Results-Oriented Performance Culture Human Capital Goal: Maintain a diverse, results-oriented, high-performing workforce and utilize a performance management system that effectively differentiates between high and low performance, linking individual/team/unit performance to organizational goals and desired results.

- Analysis of data from the 2009 Annual Employee Survey and the 2010 Employee Viewpoint Survey.

- Merit System compliance reviews of performance plans. 100 percent of performance plans were reviewed against requirements for regulatory compliance.

- Analysis of the SES performance management system in order to maintain certification.

- Analysis of the SL performance management system in order to request certification.

- Analysis of the awards program.

- Assessment of GS performance management system using OPM's PAAT.

Talent Management Human Capital Goal: Identify and address critical competency gaps; recruit, hire and retain employees with the skills necessary for mission accomplishment; and continue to strive for a diverse workforce that reflects the variety of American culture.

- Analysis of data from the 2009 Annual Employee Survey and the 2010 Employee Viewpoint Survey.

- Analysis of the Executive Development, Management Development, and Upward Mobility Programs.

- Merit System compliance reviews of staffing actions. Each case file that resulted from a hiring action was audited by the HRD specialist; the Team Leader for Recruitment and Staffing audited each certificate prior to finalizing the selection.

- Analysis of progress in implementing the HRD SWAT Team action plan.

- Analysis of barriers to streamlining the hiring process, eliminating the requirement for applicants to write narratives addressing the KSAs needed for jobs, implementing category rating, allowing applicants to apply with a resume and cover letter, notifying applicants at four points during the hiring process, and ensuring manager involvement in hiring.

- Analysis of data from OPM's applicant and manager surveys.

- Analysis of the hiring timeline.

- Analysis of the effectiveness of targeted outreach activities to attract diverse, highly qualified job applicants.

- Analysis of the NRS position as a unique requirement for carrying out mission-critical work.

- Analysis of workforce demographic data.

- Analysis of barriers to building a more diverse workforce.

- Analysis of data from the assessment of investigator competencies to identify gaps.

- Analysis of the Systems, Standards, and Metrics data.

- Analysis of End-to-End Hiring Metrics.

- Quality reviews of Official Personnel Folders (OPF) in preparation for conversion to electronic files.

- Completion of the annual training needs assessment.

Accountability Human Capital Goal: Ensure there is effective human capital management in support of the NTSB Strategic Plan.

- Identify activities for assessment of each human capital system.

- Compile assessments into the annual Human Capital Management Report.

The results of these various analyses and assessments have demonstrated that the NTSB is making progress in achieving its human capital goals. Agency-specific initiatives linked to each of the implementing systems have contributed to this progress, along with the strides being made on governmentwide initiatives to improve the hiring process, to measure and act on the perceptions of the workforce to increase employee engagement and satisfaction, and to increase telework, as well as health and wellness, as programs that lead to work/life balance and contribute to organizational effectiveness.

Section VI

Adjustments

During FY 2010, the NTSB improved the linkage between operational HRD work and human capital goals and objectives. Measures in the operating plan reflected the agency's priorities in human capital and linked accountability for their achievement to the leaders of each of the agency's offices. At the end of each quarter, the review of data to assess progress on achieving operating plan measures provided a point for reflecting on the effectiveness of the human capital goals in framing management priorities and operational work.

Accountability information was considered when actions and targets were set for implementing the Strategic Human Capital Plan in FY 2011. During the coming year, the Strategic Human Capital Plan will be updated to align with the updated agency Strategic Plan. This update will take into account the results of this assessment of the NTSB's human capital management program.

Actions for the short term emphasize closing competency gaps for staff in mission-critical occupations; continued refinement of the planning, delivery, and evaluation of training programs; continuing development of the leadership corps; ongoing involvement of managers and supervisors in workforce planning and the hiring process; continuing improvements to streamline the hiring process and improve the experience of applicants for NTSB jobs; improvements in performance management that increase communication and feedback; and full integration of assessment activities into agency business processes.